Original title:
A New Heartbeat

Copyright © 2024 Swan Charm
All rights reserved.

Author: Paulina Pähkel
ISBN HARDBACK: 978-9916-79-141-7
ISBN PAPERBACK: 978-9916-79-142-4
ISBN EBOOK: 978-9916-79-143-1

Symphony of Awakening

In the dawn of grace and light,
Hearts are stirred in gentle flight.
Voices rise, a sacred sound,
Awakening love, where peace is found.

With every breath, the spirit sings,
A melody of holy things.
Each note a whisper from above,
In harmony, we share the love.

Celestial Resurgence

Stars alight in skies so vast,
Binding futures with the past.
In silence, wisdom softly flows,
A truth that only spirit knows.

From ashes born, a rise anew,
Guided by the light so true.
In every heart, a flame ignites,
A dance of hope in sacred nights.

The Quiet Revolution of the Soul

In stillness lies the holy spark,
Transforming shadows that leave a mark.
With quiet strength, the spirit breaks,
A revolution that awakens fates.

The whispering winds of truth we feel,
In gentle ways, this change is real.
Each moment holds a chance to rise,
And dare to look beyond the skies.

Harmony in Transformation

Beneath the surface, waters churn,
In every heart, the lessons learned.
Like rivers flowing, we must change,
In every trial, we rearrange.

With every step, a path unfolds,
A story of faith, brave and bold.
Transformation in the soul's embrace,
In love's reflection, we find our place.

The Blessing of Fresh Beginnings

In dawn's embrace, new hopes arise,
Each moment whispers, a sweet, soft sigh.
Forgiveness blooms where shadows trod,
A sacred space, where love is God.

With gentle hands, we mold the day,
In faith we walk, come what may.
The past dissolves like morning mist,
In every breath, find joy's sweet kiss.

Chords of Redemption

Divine melodies weave through time,
Each soul's lament, a sacred rhyme.
With every note, we find our way,
Through trials faced, in light we sway.

Resounding truths unite us here,
In harmony, we lose the fear.
The chords of grace, they echo loud,
In faith and love, we stand unbowed.

Illuminated Path of the Heart

A lantern glows within the night,
Guiding the lost towards the light.
Each step we take, in love's embrace,
Leads us to God's most sacred space.

With open hearts, we seek to find,
The whispered truths of the divine.
In quiet moments, souls connect,
Unveiling love in pure respect.

Wings of Seraphim

In celestial realms, the seraph dance,
With wings of fire, a heavenly trance.
They sing of peace in sacred song,
Where hearts unite, and spirits long.

With every beat, the heavens soar,
Echoing love forevermore.
In their embrace, we find our flight,
Transcending shadows, embraced by light.

Wings of Change

Beneath the sky, the storm does break,
Yet from the chaos, new paths wake.
With outstretched wings, we learn to rise,
Transforming pain into the skies.

With every breath, a fresh start blooms,
In trust we step through darkened rooms.
In unity, our spirits shift,
Embracing change, our cherished gift.

Echoes of Divine Promise

In the silence of the night,
Whispers of hope arise,
The heart beats in rhythm,
With faith that never dies.

Stars gather in the heavens,
Bearing messages of light,
Each promise softly spoken,
Guiding us through the night.

As dawn breaks the horizon,
Shadows fleetingly fade,
In the warmth of His presence,
All doubts are gently laid.

Through valleys deep and wide,
His love will always stand,
With every step beside us,
We tread on promised land.

In every tear that glistens,
Is a story to be told,
Of grace that heals the broken,
And renews the weary soul.

The Awakening Pulse

In the quiet of the morn,
A gentle whisper calls,
The spirit stirs within me,
Awake, my soul enthralls.

In sunlight's warm embrace,
Life's tapestry is spun,
Each moment holds a blessing,
A journey just begun.

When burdens weigh upon me,
The heart begins to rise,
With every prayer of yearning,
We touch the boundless skies.

The call of distant mountains,
Echo within my chest,
In each beat lies a promise,
A chance to seek the blessed.

The pulse of faith, unbroken,
Resounds in every hand,
Together in His spirit,
We walk on sacred land.

Resurrection of the Inner Flame

In darkness, embers flicker,
A spark of hope is born,
Resilience in our story,
From ashes, light is worn.

Each struggle is a ripple,
In the vast sea of grace,
The flame inside is rising,
Illuminating space.

Through trials and through sorrows,
Our spirits intertwine,
In the depth of despair,
We find the strength divine.

With every act of kindness,
The fire deeper grows,
In unity and love,
A brighter path we close.

Together we are rising,
From shadows into light,
The resurrection calls us,
To shine both day and night.

Serenade of Grace Renewed

In the garden of our hearts,
A melody takes flight,
Each note sings of redemption,
In the stillness of the night.

Soft breezes carry whispers,
Of love that knows no end,
In every bloom and blessing,
The universe will mend.

With each dawn comes the promise,
Of grace that flows like streams,
In harmony, we gather,
To weave our sacred dreams.

The symphony of silence,
Calls forth the weary soul,
In the embrace of kindness,
We dance to love's sweet goal.

As nightfall gently welcomes,
The stars begin to gleam,
In the serenade of grace,
We find the dawn of dream.

Rhythms of the Spirit's Embrace

In the stillness, souls align,
A dance of faith, a light divine.
The heartbeat echoes soft and near,
In every breath, the Spirit's cheer.

Hands lifted high, we seek the way,
Through trials faced, in love we stay.
The sacred rhythm guides our heart,
In every step, we play our part.

Beneath the stars, our worries cease,
Embraced in grace, we find our peace.
Whispers of hope flow through the air,
In unity, our spirits share.

Like rivers deep, our voices blend,
A song of faith that knows no end.
In silence heard, or praises sung,
The Spirit's embrace, forever young.

With open hearts, we journey on,
Through shadows dark, into the dawn.
The rhythms pulse with life anew,
In every moment, we find you.

The Gentle Whisper of Grace

Amidst the chaos, soft and clear,
A whisper floats, dispelling fear.
Each tender note, a gift of love,
From realms unseen, to us above.

The quiet call that leads us home,
In every heart, the seeds are sown.
With every prayer, we seek the light,
The gentle whispers guide our flight.

Through trials steep, we find our way,
In moments dark, we choose to pray.
The grace we seek is ever near,
In quietude, it draws us here.

The world may fade, but love remains,
In every joy, in every pain.
With each embrace, our burdens lift,
In gentle whispers, life's true gift.

So let us listen, let us feel,
The grace that flows, a sacred seal.
In harmony, our spirits rise,
With gentle whispers, we touch the skies.

Echoes from the Divine

In the mountain's breath, we find the call,
A sacred echo, in awe we fall.
The wisdom shared, like stars that shine,
In every heart, we trace the line.

From sacred texts to hearts that sing,
The echoes weave, our souls take wing.
In silence deep, the truth revealed,
A unity that has been sealed.

Through trials faced and mountains climbed,
In harmony, our spirits rhymed.
The whispers from the past remain,
Guiding us through joy and pain.

Each moment touched, a memory bright,
In echoes heard, we find the light.
With every beat, our spirits rise,
In divine love, we claim the prize.

So let us walk this path of grace,
With open hearts, we find our place.
In every echo, we shall trust,
To guide our souls, it's truly just.

Where Spirit Meets the Pulse

In the heartbeat of the earth so wide,
The Spirit's pulse, our faithful guide.
With every step, a dance of grace,
In sacred moments, we find our space.

Through whispered prayers, we seek the way,
In unity, our hearts convey.
The rhythm flows, as time unwinds,
In every soul, the truth that binds.

The sacred ties, they intertwine,
In every pulse, love's design.
Through trials faced, we rise anew,
In every breath, we're born and grew.

As dawn breaks soft, the shadows flee,
In every heart, the Spirit's plea.
With hands uplifted, we praise the day,
Where Spirit meets, we humbly sway.

So let us join this sacred song,
Where every heart and pulse belong.
In peace we gather, side by side,
In Spirit's light, we must abide.

Rejuvenation of the Spirit's Song

In the stillness, whispers rise,
Awakening love beneath the skies.
Harmony flows, a river so deep,
As we awaken from our sleep.

Graceful melodies fill the air,
Lifted by faith, dispelling despair.
Each note a promise, soft and clear,
Guiding us closer, year by year.

With every breath, a new refrain,
Washing away the sorrow and pain.
In unity, our spirits unite,
Shining together, pure and bright.

Hearts interwoven, gentle and strong,
Together we sing the sacred song.
Rejuvenation of all that is pure,
In the spirit's embrace, we endure.

Let the echoes of love resound,
In the silence, let joy be found.
Rejuvenation is ours to claim,
Embracing the light, we rise in His name.

Sacred Breath of New Life

In the dawn's light, we take breath,
A sacred promise, life over death.
With every inhale, the soul is stirred,
In the stillness, His voice is heard.

The air, a gift of love divine,
Filling our hearts, His light will shine.
Renewal springs forth, pure and true,
In the sacred breath, we are made new.

In the garden, life's fragrance blooms,
Casting away all shadows and glooms.
With each heartbeat, a story unfolds,
Of sacred moments, age-old and bold.

Let us gather in praise and prayer,
With every exhale, our worries laid bare.
In the abundance of grace, we thrive,
With the sacred breath, we come alive.

Life a journey, cherished and sweet,
In His presence, our spirits meet.
Sacred breath ignites our way,
In the dance of new life, we sway.

The Dance of Endless Potential

In the quiet spaces, dreams take flight,
Unveiling the path from darkness to light.
With each movement, the soul expands,
In the dance of grace, we join His hands.

Steps of faith lead us through the night,
Lights of hope sparkle, brilliant and bright.
In every twirl, a promise laid,
An endless potential, never to fade.

Hearts entwined in a rhythm divine,
Together we flourish, together we shine.
Every heartbeat a symphony sweet,
In the dance of creation, we find our beat.

With open arms, we embrace the call,
In the circle of life, we rise and fall.
Movement ignites the fire within,
In the dance of potential, love will begin.

Let us sway to the music of grace,
In the journey ahead, we find our place.
The dance of life, ever so free,
In unity's spirit, we will be.

Heartstrings of Hope

With every chord, a melody born,
In the silence of night, or the break of morn.
Heartstrings awaken, vibrating with grace,
As hope dances softly, illuminating space.

In trials faced, we seek the light,
Through shadows and fears, we hold on tight.
Each note a reminder, sweet and sincere,
That even in darkness, His love is near.

Threads of compassion carefully spun,
Mapping our journey, uniting as one.
In the tapestry woven, stories collide,
Heartstrings of hope, forever our guide.

When storms may whisper and doubts may roar,
We cling to the promise of joy at the core.
In each heartbeat, the spirit will sing,
Together we rise, on hope's gentle wing.

So let love be the echo, the song in our hearts,
Guiding us always, in all of life's arts.
With heartstrings entwined, we strive and cope,
Together forever in the essence of hope.

Divine Echoes in Stillness

In the quiet, whispers call,
Hearts uplifted, we stand tall.
Grace descends like morning light,
Guiding souls through endless night.

Silent prayers sweetly soar,
Opening every sacred door.
In stillness, God's voice we hear,
Filling us with love, not fear.

Nature's breath, a holy hymn,
As shadows fade, His love runs brim.
Each moment, sacred truths arise,
In tranquil spaces, peace complies.

Beneath the stars, we find our way,
Steeping in the dawn of day.
Every echo speaks His name,
In stillness, we are never the same.

Embrace the quiet, let it be,
The soul's reflection sets us free.
In divine presence, we are whole,
United, body, spirit, soul.

The Beat of Redemption

In shadows deep, grace meets the pain,
A heart reborn, washed free from stain.
Love's anthem rises, bold and clear,
In the rhythm, hope draws near.

Though trials churn like stormy seas,
Faith stands firm, our greatest ease.
Each heartbeat whispers, 'You are known,'
In every struggle, seeds are sown.

Through valleys low, and peaks so bright,
Redemption dances in the light.
With every step, the path unfolds,
A story of love, forever told.

The past may linger, but grace renews,
In every moment, a chance to choose.
With open arms, we take the lead,
Embracing truth, fulfilling need.

So let the beat of life resound,
In every heart, His love is found.
From brokenness, we rise again,
In redemption's song, we shall remain.

A Journey to the Inner Sanctuary

Within the heart, a temple waits,
Where silence speaks to open gates.
In sacred stillness, we ascend,
To find the peace that will not end.

Each breath a prayer, each thought a light,
Guiding us through the endless night.
With every step, the spirit blooms,
In the sanctuary, love consumes.

Questions linger, yet faith prevails,
Through winding paths and gentler trails.
The inner light will show the way,
A journey bright, vibrant as day.

In meditation, truth will guide,
In every corner, He will bide.
As layers shed, the soul ignites,
In unity with sacred sights.

So trust the journey deep and wide,
With open hearts, we'll turn the tide.
To the sanctuary, we are drawn,
Where love awakens with the dawn.

Revived in Reverence

In awe we stand, before the Divine,
Where hearts align like stars that shine.
The sacred moment holds our breath,
In reverence, we conquer death.

With open palms, we seek the grace,
In every challenge, His embrace.
Transformed by love, our spirits soar,
In unity, forevermore.

Songs of faith like rivers flow,
A melody the angels know.
Each note resounds, a heavenly call,
In worship sweet, we give our all.

From ashes rise, in glory's light,
Revived in reverence, hearts ignite.
The sacred dance awakens soul,
In His presence, we are whole.

So let us gather, hands entwined,
In love's pure essence, we are aligned.
Together we'll rise, forever blessed,
In reverence deep, we find our rest.

Reverence in the Heart's Refuge

In whispers soft, the spirit speaks,
Within the heart, where silence seeks.
A sacred place, the soul finds peace,
In reverence deep, all worries cease.

With open arms, the light does flow,
In light's embrace, our spirits grow.
Among the echoes of sweet prayer,
The heart's refuge, a love so rare.

The stars above, they gently guide,
Through valleys dark, with faith beside.
In unity, our voices rise,
To worship Him who hears our cries.

With humble hearts, we seek the truth,
In grace bestowed, we find our youth.
The spirit dances, joyfully free,
In reverence deep, we honor Thee.

Blooming in the Garden of Grace

In fields of gold, the flowers sway,
Their colors bright, in dawn's soft ray.
Each petal sings a hymn of love,
In the garden blessed from above.

Amidst the thorns, the roses bloom,
With fragrant whispers, chase off gloom.
The roots of faith, they intertwine,
In sacred soil, our hearts align.

Sunlight beams on gentle streams,
Where hope is born, and life redeems.
Through seasons changing, growth will rise,
In God's embrace, we claim the prize.

With every step, the path unfolds,
A destiny in His hands holds.
In harmony, we dance and sing,
In the garden of grace, we take wing.

Cadence of Celestial Change

In twilight's glow, the heavens shift,
A tapestry of stars, a sacred gift.
With each new dawn, the world awakes,
In celestial rhythm, all hearts quake.

The moon ascends, a silver guide,
In her presence, shadows abide.
With every phase, a lesson learned,
In cycles vast, our spirits yearned.

The winds of change, they softly call,
To embrace the rise and the fall.
In every heartbeat, the dance we share,
A melody woven with tender care.

In prayerful whispers, we seek the light,
In faith's embrace, we stand upright.
With patience learned in night's long veil,
The cadence of change, a heavenly trail.

A Covenant of Renewed Life

In sacred bond, we find our strength,
Through trials faced, we go the length.
A covenant made, profound and true,
In love's embrace, we are made new.

The waters flow, with grace imbued,
With every drop, our spirits renewed.
In unity, we forge our way,
With hearts aflame, we boldly pray.

In every tear, a story sown,
Through pain and joy, we have grown.
With faith as roots, we stand as one,
A covenant sealed, when day is done.

In every sunrise, a promise clear,
The gift of life we hold so dear.
With open hearts, we rise and strive,
In the covenant of renewed life.

Breath of the Infinite

In the stillness, grace descends,
Whispers of love that never end.
Stars align in sacred light,
Guiding souls through darkest night.

Hands uplifted to the sky,
Hearts entwined as we rely.
In each breath, a promise made,
In every prayer, a path is laid.

From the depths of endless seas,
To the heights of ancient trees,
Life's journey echoes deep within,
Awakening the soul's own hymn.

Eternity's gentle call,
Invites us to rise and fall.
In the cycle, find your place,
In every moment, seek His face.

Through the trials, through the tears,
Faith endures and conquers fears.
With each heartbeat, love will flow,
A sacred bond we come to know.

A Symphony of Hope's Embrace

In the quiet, echoes swell,
Harmony in every bell.
Notes of joy and peace arise,
Filling hearts like open skies.

In the laughter, in the song,
Where the weak and lost belong.
Through the shadows, faith prevails,
Guiding ships with righteous sails.

Every tear a sacred note,
In this song, our spirits float.
Joining voices, souls entwined,
A vision of the divine kind.

With the dawn, hope's light will gleam,
In every heart, a shining dream.
Together, hand in hand we rise,
In love's embrace, we touch the skies.

Let the chorus ever sound,
In our hearts, the truth is found.
From despair, we find our way,
In this symphony, we pray.

The Dawn of Transcendence

Awakened in the morning light,
Surrendered soul takes flight.
Through the veil, we see the grace,
Of that which time cannot erase.

In the silence, wisdom cries,
To behold the endless skies.
Each moment holds a sacred truth,
Remembering the essence of youth.

With the sun, creation breathes,
Woven gently with the leaves.
In the stillness, spirits soar,
Transcending all we knew before.

Faith ignites the inner fire,
Lifting hearts, igniting desire.
In this dawn, we seek and find,
The everlasting, intertwined.

As we walk this hallowed ground,
In unity, our hearts are bound.
The dawn awakens all that's true,
In every shade, the light shines through.

Hymn of the Reborn Spirit

In the ashes, life is born,
From the dusk, behold the morn.
Rising up with courage bright,
A spirit renewed, takes flight.

With each heartbeat, a new refrain,
Through the struggle, through the pain.
In the dance of life, we learn,
Every twist, a flame we burn.

In the spirit's gentle song,
We discover where we belong.
In the depths of trials faced,
Each challenge met, a soul embraced.

Falling leaves give way to bloom,
In every heart, dispel the gloom.
Through the night, the stars will guide,
As we walk with grace and pride.

In the chorus of the kind,
Hands uplifted, hearts aligned.
Together, in this sacred place,
We find our truth, we find His grace.

Clarity in the Heart's Sanctuary

In the stillness, whispers rise,
Guided paths beneath the skies.
Each thought, a prayer softly said,
In the sanctuary where faith is bred.

Light pierces through the heavy veil,
Hope unfurls, a tender sail.
With open hearts, we seek the grace,
In every moment, we find our place.

Beyond shadows, truth shines bright,
Illuminating the darkest night.
Each heartbeat echoes the sacred call,
In unity, we rise and fall.

Hands united, we stand as one,
In this temple, life is spun.
Embrace the peace, let spirits soar,
For love is what we're truly for.

As dawn awakens, the soul ignites,
Guided by love's eternal lights.
Clarity blooms within each prayer,
In the heart's sanctuary, all is fair.

Reflections of the Divine Within

In every gaze, the spark resides,
A flicker born where love abides.
Mirrored souls, our essence beams,
In kindness, we fulfill our dreams.

With every breath, a sacred trust,
Whispers of hope rise from the dust.
In silence, we hear the spirit's song,
A dance of light where we belong.

Through trials faced, we find our way,
Strengthened by love's gentle sway.
The path unfolds with each step true,
Reflections show the divine in you.

Embrace the joy, let sorrows fade,
In the heart's embrace, all debts are paid.
Together we rise, hand in hand,
In this vast and wondrous land.

The tapestry woven, threads divine,
In every heart, a sacred sign.
Reflections whisper, 'We are one,'
In the light of love, we've just begun.

The Pulse of Eternal Hope

In the dawn, a heartbeat new,
Echoing promises, pure and true.
With every pulse, the world awakens,
Hope ignites where darkness beckons.

Within each soul, a flicker glows,
A beacon bright, as faith bestows.
Through trials faced, we rise and stand,
Together guided by loving hands.

The rhythm of life, a sacred dance,
In each heartbeat, a second chance.
Hope flows through, a river wide,
In unity, we shall abide.

With open hearts, we dare to dream,
In the fabric of life, we gleam.
Every moment holds the key,
To unlock joy and set us free.

In the pulse of time, a promise made,
In every breath, love's serenade.
No shadow long can hold us tight,
For hope, like dawn, brings endless light.

Renewal in Every Breath

Inhale the grace, exhale the pain,
Each moment new, a chance to gain.
In whispered prayers, the spirit flows,
Renewal blooms where love bestows.

The wind carries whispers of the past,
A gentle reminder that love will last.
With every sigh, we shed what's old,
In this cycle, our stories unfold.

In nature's rhythm, life's song we find,
Every heartbeat, a bond that binds.
The sun sets low, then rises high,
In the dance of time, we learn to fly.

With open hands, we greet the day,
In each little moment, we find our way.
Rebirth around us, a vibrant glow,
In every breath, love continues to flow.

As seasons change, so do we grow,
In the heart's garden, new paths we sow.
Through every trial, find strength to rise,
For renewal's beauty forever lies.

Whispers of Renewal

In the stillness, hope awakes,
Gentle breezes, love's embrace.
Nature sings of life anew,
With each dawn, our spirits grew.

Hearts aflame with sacred fire,
Guided by a deep desire.
Hands extended, reaching high,
We rise together, you and I.

Through the valleys, shadows creep,
Yet in faith, our courage leaps.
With each challenge, we find grace,
Embracing all that time can trace.

The river flows, a holy stream,
Washing over every dream.
In the journey, we are found,
With every step, love's echo sound.

So let us walk this path as one,
Underneath the rising sun.
With whispers soft, our spirits blend,
In the light, our hearts ascend.

The Sacred Pulse Within

Deep within, a rhythm beats,
Echoing where the spirit meets.
In quiet hours, truth revealed,
A sacred bond, forever sealed.

Like morning dew on blades of grass,
Moments cherished, time will pass.
Each heartbeat, a prayer in tune,
Guided by the silver moon.

With every breath, we feel the grace,
A tapestry that time can trace.
Hands clasped tight, united we stand,
A woven tale, eternally planned.

Voices rise in harmony,
Singing songs of reverie.
In the silence, all is clear,
The sacred pulse draws ever near.

So let your spirit dance and sway,
In this moment, come what may.
For in the heart, the truth we find,
A loving force that intertwines.

Rhythm of the Divine

In the dawn, a whisper calls,
Echoing through ancient halls.
Nature's song, a soothing balm,
Bringing worlds to peace and calm.

Each beat, a blessing from above,
Guided by the hand of love.
In unity, our souls align,
Moving to the rhythm divine.

Through trials faced and mountains climbed,
In every step, the heart's designed.
Together, we will reach the heights,
In the grace of endless nights.

With spirit strong, we walk our path,
Embracing joy, dispelling wrath.
In the dance of life, we find
The true essence, intertwined.

So let the rhythm guide our way,
In faith, we trust, come what may.
As one, we journey ever on,
In the light of a new dawn.

Echoes of Grace

In the silence, echoes ring,
Wisdom found in everything.
A gentle touch of the divine,
In every heart, a spark that shines.

With open arms, we welcome light,
Guiding our souls through darkest night.
With every breath, a chance to see,
The beauty in our unity.

Through trials faced and joys embraced,
In every tear, love is traced.
Finding solace in the storm,
In grace, we gather, hearts transform.

Let the echoes sing our fate,
A symphony we'll celebrate.
In every heartbeat, we proclaim,
Together we rise, unashamed.

So hear the whispers in the air,
A call to love, to deeply care.
In every moment, we will stand,
Echoes of grace, hand in hand.

When the Soul Blossoms

In silence deep, the heart awakes,
A garden blooms where mercy breaks.
Petals soft with grace align,
In every breath, the soul's design.

The whispers of the heavens sing,
In joy, the spirit finds its wing.
With open arms, we dance and sway,
To sacred truths that guide our way.

Through trials faced, the light expands,
In unity, we weave great strands.
The fragrance sweet, a love divine,
In every moment, we entwine.

As sunlit rays on autumn's grove,
Each soul awakens, stretches, rove.
The colors shine, a vibrant hue,
In gratitude, our hearts renew.

In kindness shared, we find our peace,
A gentle breeze, our burdens cease.
With faith as roots, we rise above,
Together wrapped in endless love.

Embracing the Divine Frequency

The universe hums a sacred song,
In every note, we all belong.
Vibrations lift us, hearts set free,
To dance in realms of unity.

In stillness, feel the cosmic sway,
A light so pure, it guides the way.
In waves of love, we find our place,
Embracing life, we seek its grace.

Through trials faced, through joys profound,
In every heartbeat, truth is found.
With whispers soft, the spirit leads,
In harmony, we plant the seeds.

The pulse of all creation's might,
A tapestry of day and night.
With every breath, we rise and soar,
To touch the stars, to seek much more.

In sacred circles, spirits blend,
In love's embrace, we transcend.
Together bound, in light we stand,
To weave our dreams with gentle hands.

Graced with New Beginnings

In twilight's glow, the dawn appears,
A veil is lifted, calming fears.
Each moment fresh, a chance to grow,
In faith we walk where rivers flow.

With open hearts, we greet the day,
In solitude, we learn to pray.
A chance to breathe, to start anew,
In every struggle, strength breaks through.

The sun arises, the shadows fade,
In every choice, our paths are laid.
With hands outstretched, we seek the light,
In brilliance born from darkest night.

Through trials faced, we rise and shine,
Each step a gift, each breath divine.
In every tear, a lesson learned,
In every fire, our spirits burned.

In thanksgiving, we lift our voices,
With grateful hearts, we make our choices.
Embraced by love, we find our way,
In every dawn, a brand new day.

Breathe the Light of Eternity

In breath of life, the spirit stirs,
In sacred moments, truth occurs.
To breathe the light, divine and clear,
In every pulse, we draw it near.

With open eyes, we find our peace,
In silence shared, our fears release.
Embracing all, we come alive,
Through love and grace, our souls revive.

With every sigh, we touch the stars,
In cosmic dance, we heal our scars.
Eternity whispers, soft and low,
Guiding hearts where rivers flow.

In gentle waves, we rise and fall,
In unity, we heed the call.
From shadows deep, we learn to fly,
On wings of hope, we touch the sky.

To breathe the light of all creation,
In every heart, a revelation.
Through love's embrace, we find our fate,
In every moment, we celebrate.

Celestial Awakening

In silence, the heavens call,
A whisper of grace, a view so small.
Stars ignite in the endless night,
Guiding the soul toward sacred light.

The dawn of hope begins to bloom,
Each heart rejoices, dispelling gloom.
Angelic voices, a heavenly choir,
Lift our spirits, set them higher.

Awake, arise, the time is nigh,
To seek the truth, to reach the sky.
Under the watch of celestial eyes,
We find our strength, our spirits rise.

The world transformed in the morning glow,
With every heartbeat, the love will flow.
Celestial beings, guide our flight,
In unity, we march toward the light.

With every breath, we offer praise,
In sacred moments, our souls shall raise.
Together we stand, forever bound,
In celestial truth, our faith is found.

The Song of Seraphim

From heights beyond, the seraphs sing,
In radiant chorus, their praises swing.
Hearts ablaze, they soar above,
With hymns of joy and endless love.

In the presence of the Holy One,
Each note a spark, each word a sun.
Wings of light, they cascade down,
Bestowing grace, in love we drown.

They whisper secrets of the divine,
In every prayer, their spirits entwine.
With fervent song, they lift our cries,
In heavenly realms, our hope flies.

With fiery souls and gentle grace,
They guide us through each solemn space.
In trials faced, they stand beside,
A testament of faith as our guide.

Oh, sing the song that never ends,
A melody where the heart transcends.
In unity, as one we stand,
To greet the light in this sacred land.

From Darkness to Illuminated Paths

Through shadows deep, we wander lost,
Seeking the light, we pay the cost.
In faith we tread, through nights so long,
Finding our way in the whispered song.

Each step we take, the dawn draws near,
A beacon of hope that calms our fear.
Illuminated paths await the brave,
With every choice, a soul we save.

From chains of doubt, we break away,
Into the dawn of a brand new day.
A sacred journey where shadows fade,
In love's embrace, our fears are laid.

The gentle light begins to rise,
Awakening dreams, unveiling skies.
With hearts in tune and spirits free,
We walk in grace, just you and me.

Together we shine, our spirits bold,
In the warmth of love, our story told.
From darkness deep to paths so bright,
We'll forge ahead, embraced by light.

A New Dawn of Praise

With every sunrise, a promise wakes,
A symphony of grace from the heavens aches.
The world rejoices in colors anew,
In harmony, we sing, our hearts in view.

The morning light, a gentle start,
Illuminates the depth of every heart.
In gratitude, we lift our hands,
To praise the One who understands.

Upon this earth, we gather strong,
United in faith, where we belong.
In shared belief, our spirits soar,
A testament of love forevermore.

Voices rise like incense sweet,
In every moment, we find our feet.
With gladness and joy, we take our place,
In the warmth of His unending grace.

So let us sing, the new dawn bright,
A chorus of hope, a sacred light.
In every heart, the music plays,
Forever bound in a new dawn of praise.

Heartstrings of Faith

In shadowed nights, I seek the light,
A whisper from the realm so bright.
Each prayer I send in hopes to grace,
Guides my heart to a holy place.

With every tear, a lesson learned,
In trials faced, my spirit burned.
Yet in the pain, new strength I find,
A bond of love that's intertwined.

Through storms that rage, I stand so tall,
For in my heart, I've heard the call.
With faith as my anchor, I won't sway,
In trust, I walk, come what may.

In silence deep, His voice will sound,
In every beat, the grace I've found.
With open arms, His love does flow,
A sacred path, I gladly know.

So let the heartstrings play their song,
In unity, we all belong.
For faith, a guide, forever stays,
In endless love, our spirits praise.

The Melody of Second Chances

In echoes soft, redemption sings,
A gentle touch, the hope it brings.
Each stumble leads to paths anew,
In grace, our souls are born anew.

The trials faced, a forging fire,
Through darkest nights, we find desire.
With every fall, we rise again,
In love's embrace, we feel no pain.

A second chance, a whispered call,
To rise again, we must not fall.
With open hearts, forgiveness flows,
In every note, a promise grows.

Together bound, we share the weight,
In unity, we celebrate.
For second chances, bright and clear,
Transforming doubt to joy sincere.

So let the melody resound,
In every soul, true hope is found.
Through harmony, we understand,
In every heart, we make our stand.

Divine Rhythm of Creation

In every dawn, the world awakes,
A dance of light, the beauty makes.
The stars align in cosmic flow,
In nature's heart, the wonders show.

The mountains rise, a testament,
To love's embrace, forever sent.
In rivers' song, a sacred pulse,
The rhythm of life, vast and vast.

From every grain, the earth's embrace,
In silent prayer, we find our place.
With hands uplifted, we create,
A masterpiece, our hearts elate.

The colors blend in every hue,
A tapestry of love so true.
In every breath, creation sings,
A timeless dance, the joy it brings.

As night falls soft, we gather near,
In awe of all the life we share.
For in this space, we come alive,
In divine rhythm, we will thrive.

The Sacred Tune of Awakening

In quiet moments, whispers rise,
A sacred tune beneath the skies.
Awakening hearts to truth's embrace,
In every note, we find our place.

With open eyes, the world unfurls,
A melody that softly swirls.
In every breath, the spirit grows,
A light within, forever glows.

The call to rise, it echoes clear,
In loving arms, we have no fear.
Through trials passed, we stand as one,
In unity, our battles won.

Each step we take, a dance of grace,
In every heartbeat, love's embrace.
With faith as guide, we journey on,
To sacred tunes, our hearts respond.

So let us sing this song of light,
In harmony, we shine so bright.
With every dawn, new hope we find,
In sacred tunes, our souls entwined.

Unseen Hands and Shimmering Hues

In the silence of the dawn's embrace,
Unseen hands weave a sacred space.
With shimmering hues that dance and sway,
Life's gentle whispers beckon to pray.

Light cascades in patterns divine,
Guiding souls on paths that align.
Through trials and storms, we find our way,
Held by the love that will never stray.

In shadows cast by worldly fears,
The unseen hands wipe away the tears.
Each shimmer a promise, a sacred sign,
Faith in the journey, a heart that shines.

Through every moment, tender and true,
Unseen hands shape all that we pursue.
In shimmering hues, the world we see,
An echo of grace, profound and free.

Embrace the light, let spirits soar,
Guided by love, forevermore.
In unseen hands, our hopes reside,
Shimmering hues, a faithful guide.

Echoes of the Eternal

In the stillness, echoes arise,
Whispers of truth beneath the skies.
A symphony played on heaven's strings,
As the heart awakens, eternal springs.

Voices of ages call to the soul,
Each note a memory, making us whole.
From shadows we come, to brightness we tread,
Echoes of love, where angels have led.

In the depths of night, a flicker of grace,
Guiding the lost to a sacred space.
With every heartbeat, the past intertwines,
In echoes of the eternal, our spirit shines.

Through valleys of doubt, through mountains of faith,
The echoes resound, displaying our fate.
With every breath, we are called to see,
The eternal dance, forever free.

In each prayer whispered, in each tear shed,
The echoes of light, where we are led.
To the infinite realm, where love is the way,
Echoes of the eternal guide our stay.

Renewal in the Morning Glow

At dawn's first light, a promise reborn,
In the morning glow, a new day is sworn.
Each ray a caress, a gentle embrace,
Renewal unfolds in this sacred place.

The darkness of night fades softly away,
As whispers of hope greet the new day.
In every moment, we rise and we flow,
Singing the hymns of the morning glow.

Nature awakens, her beauty revealed,
In the vibrant colors, our hearts are healed.
With every sunrise, we stand juxtaposed,
In renewal's arms, the spirit is posed.

Through trials of yesterday, we find our strength,
As we walk in light, we cherish the length.
In love's gentle rhythm, we dance to and fro,
Basking in warmth, in the morning glow.

With gratitude rising, our spirits take flight,
In the dawn's embrace, we embrace the light.
Each day a canvas, with colors to show,
Our hearts painted bright in the morning glow.

The Melody of Graceful Rebirth

In quiet corners where shadows reside,
The melody plays, both gentle and wide.
With notes of compassion that tenderly flow,
Whispers of grace in the heartbeat below.

A symphony woven with threads of the past,
Each moment a measure, both soft and steadfast.
In cycles of life, we learn how to dance,
The melody beckons, a soulful romance.

From ashes we rise, like the phoenix in flight,
Embracing the dawn, emerging from night.
The cadence of love pulses deep in our core,
In the melody's arms, we seek to explore.

With each gentle note, the heart finds its way,
A rhythm of kindness we bring to the day.
In graceful rebirth, we rise and we yearn,
For the melody's truth, we patiently learn.

Harmony builds in the spaces between,
In the melody's embrace, we find what is unseen.
With each breath a song, we find our rebirth,
In the dance of the cosmos, we discover our worth.

The Blessing of Fresh Starts

In dawn's embrace, the new day waits,
A whisper of hope, as darkness abates.
With every breath, a promise reborn,
The heart awakens, no longer forlorn.

Grace flows gently, a river of light,
Guiding the weary through sorrow's night.
In every moment, a chance to renew,
The sacred path leads me back to You.

With faith as my anchor, I rise from the fall,
A testament to love, I heed the call.
In trials faced, Your mercy I find,
Wisdom unveiled, with a loving mind.

Joy springs forth in the fields of despair,
You paint the skies with colors so rare.
The blessing of fresh starts, a divine gift,
In Your embrace, my spirit finds lift.

I walk in gratitude, steps ever so light,
With You as my compass, I embrace the light.
A journey unfolding, with love as my chart,
Forever and always, a fresh, blessed start.

Resonance of the Spirit

In the silence, whispers of grace,
The spirit dances, finds its own space.
In moments still, a truth softly calls,
Within the heart, the sacred enthralls.

Each beat a prayer, resonating clear,
Echoes of love, drawing ever near.
The soul awakens to harmony's song,
In sacred rhythm, where all belong.

In every breath, a connection divine,
Threads of the cosmos in perfect design.
Together we rise, hand in hand we sway,
Resonance of truth lights our way.

Through trials faced, our spirits unite,
In the darkest hours, we seek the light.
With love as our anchor, we shall not break,
For in this melody, our hearts awake.

Together we'll journey, through storm and calm,
Resting in faith, finding strength in the balm.
The resonance of spirit, forever won't cease,
In sacred communion, we find our peace.

The Heart's Sacred Commission

With every heartbeat, a mission unfolds,
A tapestry woven with threads of gold.
The heart's sacred call, a beacon divine,
In service of love, our spirits align.

Through compassion's touch, we share our grace,
In every kindness, we find our place.
The heart's sacred commission, a path we embrace,
In giving, we gather the warmth of His face.

Each gesture a blessing, a voice from above,
Leading us onward, to act in pure love.
With open hearts, we mend what is frayed,
In unity strong, no debt left unpaid.

In trials and triumphs, we stand side by side,
With courage and faith, our hearts open wide.
The sacred commission, our legacy bright,
Forever guided by faith and by light.

Together we journey, through valleys and peaks,
In the heart's sacred mission, the spirit speaks.
For love is the answer, the truth that we share,
In this holy calling, we rise through prayer.

Transcendence in Every Beat

In the pulse of life, a rhythm does flow,
A dance of the soul, where love's essence glows.
In each fleeting moment, transcendence we seek,
With every heartbeat, the divine we speak.

Time whispers softly, the sacred unknown,
In unity's bond, we're never alone.
The echoes of laughter, the tears that we shed,
In shared experience, love's threads are fed.

Every heartbeat a story, a sacred refrain,
Connecting us souls in joy and in pain.
Transcendence is found in the simplest things,
In kindness and grace, the joy that it brings.

In the quiet of night, when the world slows its pace,
Transcendence whispers, filling empty space.
With hearts interwoven in the tapestry bright,
We catch glimpses of heaven, reflecting Your light.

So let us embrace this divine symphony,
In harmony moving, together we'll be.
For in every beat, a connection's reprieve,
Transcendence we find, in love we believe.

Illuminating the Darkness Within

In shadows deep, a light does glow,
A whisper of grace, a softening flow.
Through trials faced, the spirit soars,
Reviving the heart, opening doors.

With every tear that softly falls,
A lesson learned, divinity calls.
In quiet moments, we find our way,
Guided by faith, come what may.

The night is long, but dawn will break,
A promise held for our own sake.
Embrace the light that's deep within,
Let the healing of love begin.

When burdens weigh, and paths are steep,
Hold onto hope, your soul to keep.
For darkness fades where love takes hold,
The heart grows warm, the spirit bold.

So trust the journey, bright and wide,
With faith as your compass, love as your guide.
In every heart, the light doth shine,
Illuminating the divine.

Threads of Faith in the Fabric of Life

In woven strands of joy and pain,
A tapestry rich where hope will reign.
Each thread a story, a vibrant hue,
Binding us close, in all we do.

Through trials faced, we stand as one,
In faith united, battles won.
With every stitch, a prayer we weave,
In love's embrace, we learn to believe.

The fabric of life, both fragile and strong,
In every heartbeat, we all belong.
Let grace be the dye that colors our day,
As threads of faith guide our way.

In moments of doubt, let courage arise,
Woven with wonder, under the skies.
Each fiber a journey, sacred and true,
In the quilt of existence, it's me and you.

So hold onto faith, let it not fray,
For in unity, we find the way.
Threads of love knit us near,
In the fabric of life, we persevere.

A Heart Resounding in Solitude

In silence deep, the spirit sings,
A heart resounding with ancient things.
In moments alone, we learn to see,
The whispers of truth that set us free.

With every sigh that breaks the still,
The soul awakens, bends to will.
In quietude, the light is born,
Renewing hope with each new dawn.

The solitude a sacred space,
Where grace unfolds and fills with grace.
In every heartbeat, a prayer takes flight,
A dance with the stars, a bond with the night.

Through seasons of doubt, the heart holds strong,
In quiet resolve, we find where we belong.
Each breath a mantra, a sacred sound,
In the depths of loneliness, love is found.

So cherish the stillness, let it be,
A pathway carved for you and me.
In the solitude, we rise and grow,
A heart resounding, a softened glow.

Miracles in Metaphors of Change

In every heartbeat, a story unfolds,
Miracles hidden in moments bold.
Change is the canvas, life is the brush,
Creating beauty in the quiet hush.

From ashes arise a phoenix of light,
Transforming the dark into brilliant sight.
With every dawn, a chance to renew,
In the dance of change, we find what is true.

Each moment whispers a lesson profound,
In the chaos of life, stillness is found.
Like rivers that flow, we bend and we sway,
In metaphors lived, we discover the way.

So trust in the journey, embrace the unknown,
For in every challenge, our spirits have grown.
In the tapestry woven, we join hand in hand,
Miracles waiting, just as they've planned.

Let love be the compass, guiding your heart,
With faith as our anchor, let's never depart.
In the symphony of change, we hear the refrain,
Miracles echo, love conquers the pain.

A Breath of Spiritual Rebirth

In the stillness, a whisper calls,
From skies above, where the Spirit falls.
Awakened hearts, a moment to see,
In grace we find, our true decree.

Beneath the shadow, hope ignites,
Casting away the darkest nights.
With every breath, new life we take,
In sacred light, the soul shall wake.

Through trials deep, our faith shall rise,
As dawn unfolds in painted skies.
Each tear we've shed, a lesson learned,
For in our hearts, the fire burns.

A journey long, we walk in prayer,
Hand in hand, our burdens share.
With open hearts, we mend the seams,
Embracing life, and all its dreams.

In unity, our spirits blend,
To love, to serve, we shall extend.
In this rebirth, the past released,
In every soul, the joy increased.

Illuminated Beginnings

In twilight's glow, the shadows fade,
A path of light, divinely laid.
With steadfast faith, we take our place,
In every dawn, we meet His grace.

The sacred moments resonate,
In silence, love shall navigate.
The heart expands, the spirit soars,
Awakening truths behind closed doors.

Among the stars, a guiding hand,
Unfolding dreams, like grains of sand.
As morning breaks, our doubts release,
In every heartbeat, find our peace.

Through winding streets, we walk in trust,
With each step forward, we adjust.
For every end, a new start calls,
In love's embrace, the spirit sprawls.

In each encounter, blessings flow,
In laughter shared, our spirits grow.
Illuminated, we see the path,
In every heartbeat, love's aftermath.

The Holy Rhythm of Change

In whispered winds, the spirit moves,
Through life's cadence, love improves.
With every pulse, we dance in grace,
Embracing rhythms, time can trace.

From darkness blooms the brightest flower,
In each moment, within the hour.
Transcending fears, we rise anew,
In trust's embrace, we find our view.

With every challenge, wisdom grows,
The sacred flow, the heart bestows.
As seasons change, so do our ways,
In every sunset, hope displays.

Through sacred beats, we find our song,
In unity, where we belong.
As life unfolds, let voices blend,
In love's direction, we shall transcend.

With open arms, we greet the dawn,
For every day, a new song's drawn.
In holy rhythm, hearts align,
In every breath, the love divine.

Sacred Pulses of Creation

In every heartbeat, life begins,
A symphony where love amends.
The sacred dance of earth and sky,
In every moment, spirits fly.

Through sacred whispers, truth unfolds,
In quiet strength, we seek the bold.
With joy we walk, hand in hand,
In every step, a promise grand.

Awash in colors, life's embrace,
In harmony, we find our place.
As rivers flow, our worries cease,
In nature's arms, we find our peace.

With every dawn, creation sings,
Awakening hope on gentle wings.
In sacred pulses, life's thread we weave,
A tapestry the heart believes.

In unity, our spirits rise,
Underneath the endless skies.
For in each heartbeat, love's refrain,
Is the sacred pulse, that shall remain.

The Journey from Ashes to Abundance

From ashes we rise, in hope we unite,
The spirit ignites, dispelling the night.
With faith as our guide, we traverse the way,
To promise and bounty, in light of the day.

In trials we learn, in pain we find peace,
The blessings of hardship, our burdens release.
With eyes set on grace, we gather our heart,
For every new dawn, is a brand new start.

Embracing the depths, the shadows we face,
We seek after wisdom, in love's warm embrace.
Each step is a prayer, in silence we speak,
The journey of life, from ashes to peak.

The harvest we reap, is sown in the ground,
With seeds of our hopes, in the love that we've found.
The winds of the spirit, they carry us high,
From ashes we soar, like the eagle in the sky.

A tapestry woven, with threads of His might,
In joy we are gathered, a radiant sight.
From ashes to abundance, we rise and proclaim,
The glory of grace, in His holy name.

Voices of the Crossroad

At the crossroad's bend, we pause and reflect,
The whispers of heaven, in choices affect.
With paths that diverge, both tempting and true,
The voice of our spirit guides all that we do.

In moments of silence, the truth becomes clear,
A calling that echoes, so tender, so near.
We ponder the call, and the paths soon ahead,
With faith as our compass, by love we are led.

The burden of doubt, we lay at His feet,
For strength in surrender, our fears retreat.
The crossroads of life, where miracles bloom,
In moments of chaos, we conquer the gloom.

Each choice that we make, a ripple in time,
To nurture the spirit, to reach for the climb.
Voices of wisdom, in harmony raise,
Awakening hearts, we sing Him our praise.

In unity gathered, we measure our steps,
With hearts intertwined, as we stand on the depths.
The journey continues, our spirits in song,
At the crossroad we know, with Him we belong.

The Unfurling of Spirit's Song

In silence it starts, a whisper in night,
The spirit's soft melody, gentle and bright.
It dances within, in rhythms divine,
Unfurling in beauty, like grapevines entwine.

Each note a reflection of love's warm embrace,
In harmony echoing, we find our true place.
With voices united, we sing from the heart,
The unfurling of spirit, a sacred art.

Through valleys of sorrow, through mountains of grace,
The song carries hope, with its tender embrace.
In trials we grow, through the darkness we tread,
The spirit awakens, each fear we shed.

With each rising dawn, a new chorus flows,
Creating a symphony where His glory grows.
The language of love, in the heart it ignites,
An unfurling of spirit, in purest of lights.

Together we gather, in song we rejoice,
Moving with purpose, united our voice.
As the spirit unfurls, we rise and we shine,
Forever in harmony, our souls intertwine.

Genesis of Grace

In the beginning, a whisper was shared,
The creation of love, divinely prepared.
With breath of the Spirit, in quiet repose,
Genesis of grace, where mercy bestows.

The dawn of the world, a canvas anew,
Each stroke of compassion, in every hue.
From chaos we form, in His image we grow,
In unity bound, with a light that will glow.

With each moment crafted, by love's gentle hand,
We rise from despair, together we stand.
The seeds of forgiveness, in hearts they are sown,
The genesis of grace, where faith has been grown.

Through trials and triumphs, the seasons they change,
In lessons of life, we dance and we range.
The story unfolds, in His will and design,
In the genesis of grace, our lives intertwine.

As the horizon beckons, we journey anew,
In the genesis of grace, all things are made true.
With hearts wide awake, we embrace the embrace,
For every beginning, is rooted in grace.

A Chorus of Timeless Love

In the stillness of the dawn,
Hearts unite in sacred song,
Every note a whisper true,
Binding souls where we belong.

With every step upon this earth,
We gather strength from love's embrace,
In harmony, we find our worth,
Reflections of the divine grace.

The stars above in velvet skies,
Sing praises to the One we seek,
In silence, our spirits rise,
In joy, our voices gently speak.

Through trials faced, we hold the light,
A beacon in the darkest night,
Together, we shall stand and fight,
For love is pure and ever bright.

In every heart, a flame anew,
A chorus, vast and ever true,
In timeless love, we find our way,
Our souls entwined, come what may.

The Lightness of Being Divine

In the glow of morning's grace,
We dance upon a sacred space,
Each heartbeat sings a gentle rhyme,
Reflecting love that knows no time.

As golden rays emerge to play,
They whisper secrets of the day,
In every breath, a promise lies,
To lift us closer to the skies.

With open hearts, we cast aside,
The burdens that we often hide,
And in the light, we find our song,
In union, where we all belong.

As stars align in night's embrace,
We find our strength in love's soft face,
Eternal light that shines within,
A symphony of where we've been.

Together, we shall rise anew,
In the lightness of being true,
A journey carved through sacred time,
In every soul, a spark divine.

In the Light of Renewal

As winter fades, spring's kiss arrives,
In colors bright, our spirit thrives,
Each blossom tells a tale of grace,
In the light of our sacred space.

With every dawn, the world awakes,
In hope renewed, our heart partakes,
Transforming pain to vibrant joy,
In love's embrace, we find our buoy.

The gentle rain, a cleansing sign,
In every droplet, love divine,
We shed the past, embrace the now,
In gratitude, we humbly bow.

With open arms, we greet the sun,
A celebration of all we've won,
In the light of renewal bright,
We find our path, our guiding light.

Together, let our spirits soar,
In unity, we rise once more,
With every heartbeat, a fresh start,
In the light of love, we play our part.

Whispers from the Soul's Altar

In quiet moments, whispers call,
Messages from the heart of all,
In stillness, we find sacred truth,
An echo of our vibrant youth.

Beneath the stars, we lay our fears,
In twilight's glow, we shed our tears,
Each droplet tells a story dear,
A testament to love sincere.

The sacred flame, it flickers bright,
Guiding us through the darkest night,
A beacon of hope, forever strong,
In unity, we share our song.

With every breath, we honor grace,
In every step, we find our place,
Together, we rise and embrace,
The whispers from the soul's embrace.

In harmony, let spirits blend,
With open hearts, we shall transcend,
For on this journey, hand in hand,
We walk in faith, forever planned.

The Light Breaking Through

In shadows deep, His presence glows,
A beacon bright, where hope bestows.
Each dawn unfolds with gentle grace,
As whispers weave in sacred space.

Through trials faced, He shines anew,
With every breath, His love shines through.
The heart awakens, fears take flight,
In faith, we see the breaking light.

From darkest nights to radiant morn,
In quiet trust, the soul is born.
With every step, the path is clear,
For in His arms, we have no fear.

The world may falter, storms may rise,
Yet in His gaze, the spirit flies.
Each moment held, a gift divine,
With every heartbeat, love's design.

Together we stand, hand in hand,
United forth, a faithful band.
For in His light, we find our way,
A sacred truth, come what may.

Heart's Resilience in God's Embrace

Amidst the trials, He holds us close,
In gentle silence, our Spirit grows.
Through every tear, His warmth will stay,
A heartbeat strong, come what may.

In echoes soft, His promise flows,
Through darkest nights, His love bestows.
With every breath, our strength renewed,
In His embrace, our souls are moved.

When burdens weigh and fears surround,
In faith we rise, on holy ground.
Each moment given, a step in trust,
In God's great love, we rise, we must.

Our spirits soar on wings of grace,
In trials faced, we seek His face.
Resilient hearts, held in His light,
In every struggle, hope ignites.

Together we dance through pain and strife,
In faith we find the breath of life.
With open hearts, we stand as one,
In God's embrace, we are reborn.

Mosaic of the Spirit's Renewal

Each shard of light, a story told,
In brokenness, we find the gold.
The spirit weaves a tapestry,
In colors bright, divinity.

Through trials faced, we're shaped anew,
In every crack, His love shines through.
A mosaic built with grace divine,
Reflecting beauty, forever thine.

With hands held high, we rise in praise,
A symphony of hope displays.
For every wound, a healing touch,
In God's great love, we've gained so much.

Each piece aligns, a sacred dance,
In joy we find our second chance.
Together bound, with hearts aglow,
Embracing all, we learn and grow.

In unity, our spirits bloom,
Dispelling all the shades of gloom.
A mosaic bright, His love we know,
In every heart, compassion flows.

The Echoing Call of Grace

In whispered winds, His call is near,
A gentle nudge, dispelling fear.
Through every heart, His voice will sing,
A melody of love, He brings.

With every trial, His hand we seek,
In moments weak, we find the meek.
His grace abounds, both strong and free,
A beacon bright for you and me.

When paths are lost and nights are long,
In faith we rise, we'll carry on.
The echoing call, a sacred sound,
A rhythm sweet, in Him we're found.

Each step we take, we walk in light,
In darkened days, we find our sight.
His grace, our strength, forever stays,
A journey blessed in endless ways.

Together we gather, hearts entwined,
In sacred circles, love defined.
With open arms, we welcome grace,
In every soul, we find His face.

The Celestial Beat in Our Chests

In the quiet of dawn, the heart awakes,
Whispers of grace in every heartbeat,
Songs of the heavens echo and sing,
Binding us close to the Divine's embrace.

Stars above shimmer with hope,
Guiding our paths through shadows and light,
Each moment a gift, a sacred chance,
To dance in the rhythm of eternal truth.

With each breath, we lift our praise,
The spirit soars, unchained and free,
We join the chorus of angels bright,
In the celestial beat that lives in we.

Through trials and tears, we find our way,
Faith like the river, steady and deep,
In the hearts that love, divinity thrives,
With every pulse, the promise we keep.

Gathered in worship, souls intertwine,
The sacred path leads us hand in hand,
In the symphony of grace, we find our peace,
The celestial beat in our hearts will stand.

Grace Descends Like Morning Dew

Every dawn a promise, soft and near,
Grace descends like dew on the grass,
Tender whispers cleanse the weary soul,
Lifting our hearts as shadows pass.

Sunrise paints the world with gold,
Renewal unfolds, a gift of the light,
In each droplet rests mercy's touch,
Dancing in glory, hope takes flight.

The humble bow, recognizing grace,
Colors of love rain down from above,
In the stillness, we find our way,
Surrounded by mercy, wrapped in love.

Through trials we bloom, like flowers in spring,
Hearts unfurling beneath heaven's gaze,
We rise in faith, within each moment,
Grace descends, our spirits ablaze.

With thankful hearts, we gather near,
In the sacred, we find our place,
Bound by the dew that nourishes life,
Together we dance in the warmth of grace.

New Wings of the Spirit's Flight

Within our hearts, a spark ignites,
New wings unfurl, ready to soar,
Spirit's whispers guide us high,
Leading us to love forevermore.

Through trials faced, we shed the old,
Casting aside what held us tight,
In every ending, a new beginning,
As we embrace the spirit's flight.

Together we rise, united as one,
Hearts ablaze with heavenly fire,
In the dance of hope, we take to the skies,
Driven by love, we reach ever higher.

Each moment a journey, divine and true,
Wings of faith carry us far and wide,
We touch the heavens, our dreams awake,
In the spirit's embrace, we forever abide.

Let us honor the gift of each breath,
With gratitude sung in every voice,
In the light of the dawn, we find our way,
New wings of spirit inspire our choice.

Dance of the Soul's Rebirth

In twilight's glow, the soul begins,
A dance of life, where sorrow yields,
With every step, we shed the past,
Embraced by love, our spirit healed.

The rhythm of grace echoes within,
Hearts intertwine, a sacred bond,
In the circle of light, we rise once more,
Joined together, our spirits respond.

Every heartbeat sings a melody,
Notes of redemption flow through the air,
In the dance of rebirth, we find our truth,
Trusting the journey, alive and aware.

Let joy resound, let courage lead,
In the sacred spiral, we twirl and spin,
For in every ending, new life begins,
A dance of the soul, where love shall win.

With each graceful turn, we honor the past,
Embracing the present, our spirits entwined,
In the sacred dance, we are reborn,
In the joy of our hearts, true freedom we find.

The Beatific Awakening

In stillness of the night, we pray,
Awakening the soul to light.
Hearts alight with hopeful grace,
In His love, we find our place.

As dawn breaks, the shadows flee,
In His embrace, we are set free.
With each breath, a sacred song,
Together, we shall all belong.

The spirit soars on wings of peace,
In His presence, troubles cease.
Love ignites, a holy flame,
Forever singing of His name.

With faith renewed, we rise each day,
Guided by His gentle way.
Walk the path, both pure and bright,
For in His truth, we find our light.

So let our voices fill the skies,
Proclaiming love that never dies.
In unity, we stand as one,
Embracing mercy, till we're done.

Embrace of the Everlasting

When shadows gather, we shall call,
To Him who watches over all.
Embrace the grace that knows no end,
In His comfort, hearts ascend.

Through trials faced, we find our way,
With faith that lights our darkest day.
In every tear and every plea,
His love, a vast eternity.

Above the storms, His voice we hear,
A whisper soft, dispelling fear.
Together, we shall rise anew,
As hope returns, our souls break through.

In unity, our burdens share,
A tapestry of love and care.
Let kindness flow from every heart,
Each soul a precious work of art.

With open arms, the Savior waits,
To guide us through Heaven's gates.
In His embrace, we find our home,
In every heart, His love has grown.

The Dawn of Faith's Renewal

In the quiet morn, dawn appears,
A promise held through all our years.
Faith awakens, a gentle rise,
In every heart, a sweet surprise.

With every step, we seek the light,
Drawing strength from endless might.
A journey shared with all we meet,
Together, we are incomplete.

The sun ascends, a golden grace,
Illuminating every face.
In His truth, we stand so tall,
In unity, we hear the call.

As shadows fade, new hope shall grow,
In every heart, His love we show.
A renewed spirit, forever blessed,
In every moment, we find rest.

Let every soul sing out in praise,
To Him who guides our every gaze.
The dawn unfolds, a sacred chance,
We rise in joy, a holy dance.

A Psalm of Life Restored

From ashes rise, the spirit sings,
Resurrection, hope that springs.
In faith renewed, we find our way,
In every night, a brand new day.

With gentle hands, He holds our fears,
Cradling every joy and tear.
He binds our wounds, restores our soul,
In His embrace, we all are whole.

Each fleeting moment, a gift bestowed,
With love, our paths, He has bestowed.
In every struggle, grace will flow,
In unity, our spirits grow.

So sing, O hearts, of love divine,
In praise and worship, brightly shine.
For every trial brings us near,
To Him, our Savior, ever dear.

Through valleys low, to mountains high,
We walk with faith, and never shy.
In every breath, His truth shall soar,
A psalm of life, forevermore.

From Shadows to Radiance

In the quiet of night, a whisper calls,
Guiding the heart through shadowed halls.
The dawn breaks forth, a promise bright,
Illuminating paths with holy light.

Each tear we shed, a sacred prayer,
Lifting our souls to the heavens' care.
From depths of sorrow, rise to grace,
In love's embrace, we find our place.

The sun ascends, golden and true,
Casting away the darkness we knew.
With faith as our anchor, we stand strong,
In the chorus of angels, we belong.

Blessed are those who walk the way,
With hearts ablaze, in the light of day.
From shadows deep, our spirits soar,
In radiance found, forevermore.

Let our voices rise, a hymn resound,
In unity's strength, our hearts unbound.
For in this journey, we're never alone,
From shadows to radiance, we are home.

Tapestry of Divine Interlude

Each thread we weave, a story told,
In colors bright, and threads of gold.
The loom of faith, with each gentle hand,
Creates a vision, a holy strand.

Moments of grace, like petals rain,
Adorning our souls, healing the pain.
In silence shared, hearts intertwined,
A tapestry of love, divinely aligned.

Seek ye the truth in whispers low,
In every heartbeat, the spirit's glow.
The patterns of life, intricate and wide,
A gift from above, in love we abide.

Through trials faced, the fabric frays,
Yet strength is found in faith's embrace.
With each new dawn, we stitch anew,
A tapestry bright, reflecting the true.

Let kindness flow, like rivers wide,
In this divine interlude, we abide.
Together we rise, a chorus made,
In God's great design, our fears allayed.

The Restoration of Sacred Dreams

In twilight's glow, dreams softly fade,
Yet in the shadows, hope is laid.
With gentle hands, the heart's repair,
Restores the vision, awakens prayer.

Beneath the stars, we gather near,
In whispers soft, the path is clear.
Every challenge, a chance to grow,
In faith's embrace, love's light shall show.

The sacred flame, it flickers low,
Yet in our souls, the embers glow.
Each prayer a seed, in soil divine,
Blooming forth in God's grand design.

With hearts entwined, we'll rise once more,
From depths of doubt, to the heavens' door.
In unity's strength, our dreams revive,
Together in spirit, we truly thrive.

Let the dawn bring forth a holy scheme,
For we are one in the sacred dream.
Through trials faced, together we stand,
In restoration's light, we hold His hand.

Spiritual Revival at the Heart's Core

The ember's glow ignites the night,
A spark of hope, a guiding light.
In silence deep, the spirit wakes,
A call to love, as the dawn breaks.

With open hearts, we seek the way,
In every moment, His love will sway.
The pulse of grace, a rhythm pure,
In spiritual revival, we are sure.

Each gentle prayer, a song we share,
Binding our souls in a sacred prayer.
With joy we rise, hand in hand,
In unity's strength, forever we stand.

In valleys low, and mountains high,
The spirit moves, teaching us to fly.
With faith as our guide, we shall explore,
The depths of love at the heart's core.

Together we'll walk, through trials and strife,
In the embrace of love, we find our life.
For in this revival, our souls will soar,
In the light of the Spirit, forevermore.

From Ashes to Light

In shadows deep where hope once slept,
A whisper stirs, the silence wept,
From ashes bare, a flame ignites,
In grief's embrace, the soul takes flight.

From trials faced, a strength reborn,
In every heart, the light is worn,
Through midnight's veil, the dawn appears,
With faith as guide, we shed our fears.

The path of thorns, it leads us true,
In every tear, His love breaks through,
Embrace the scars, let them bestow,
A radiant grace that helps us grow.

Beyond the pain, the spirit's flight,
In every soul, a promise bright,
From ashes low, to heaven's rise,
In love we soar, toward the skies.

So let us walk, hand in hand,
In His embrace, we understand,
Through every storm, our hearts unite,
From ashes dark, we claim the light.

Divine Cadence of Renewal

In stillness found, the grace descends,
The whispers soft where silence bends,
A symphony of life unfolds,
In every breath, God's love enfolds.

The rhythmic pulse of stars at night,
Calls forth the truth, ignites the light,
In nature's song, we find the clue,
Each note a promise, pure and true.

Through seasons lost, we learn to grow,
In every fall, the heart will know,
Each rise anew, a sacred chance,
To join the dance, the holy dance.

Awake, my soul, the morning glows,
In every step, the spirit flows,
With open hearts, we hear the call,
United in the love of all.

So let the cadence guide our way,
In every night, there comes the day,
Through trials faced, we find our peace,
In divine rhythm, sweet release.

Chronicles of the Faithful Heart

With every heartbeat, stories weave,
In trials faced, we learn to believe,
The faithful heart, a steadfast guide,
In love's embrace, we shall abide.

Through journeys long, and paths unknown,
In every choice, His grace is shown,
The chronicles of lives we've led,
In pages turned, our hopes are spread.

Through deserts dry, the spirit calls,
In shadows cast, His light enthralls,
With every tear, a lesson learned,
In every joy, our hearts are burned.

So write your tale, with ink of grace,
In every trial, find your place,
The faithful heart, a light so bright,
In unity, we seek the right.

And as we journey, hand in hand,
Together strong, we make our stand,
For every chapter, love imparts,
The chronicles of faithful hearts.

The Awakening of the Beloved

In slumber deep, the spirit wakes,
A gentle call, in silence breaks,
Awakened to the love divine,
In every breath, the souls entwine.

Through night's embrace, we find our way,
In shadows cast, there comes the day,
With open arms, we greet the morn,
From brokenness, a new hope's born.

The tender touch, the whispers sweet,
In every heart, His presence beats,
Awake, Beloved, rise and shine,
In love's embrace, our souls align.

Each moment lived, a sacred gift,
In every trial, the spirit lifts,
With joy unbound, we dance anew,
Awakening in love's pure view.

So let us soar, on wings of grace,
In every step, we find His face,
The awakening, a journey true,
In every heart, His love shines through.

The Alchemy of the Spirit

In silence we surrender, the heart lays bare,
Transforming earthly burdens into divine air.
Golden light surrounds us, a sacred embrace,
In the furnace of love, we find our place.

With every prayer whispered, the spirit ignites,
Casting shadows of doubt into heavenly lights.
The soul, like a phoenix, rises anew,
In the alchemy of grace, we are made true.

From ashes of sorrow, the joy will arise,
A testament of faith that reaches the skies.
Each moment a miracle, each breath a song,
In the dance of the spirit, we ever belong.

The journey unfolds with each step of trust,
In the chalice of love, our spirits adjust.
Through trials and tribulations, we learn to soar,
In the alchemy of the spirit, forever more.

As rivers of wisdom flow deep in our hearts,
We gather the fragments, where peace imparts.
With hands raised in reverence, we offer our will,
In the furnace of faith, our souls are fulfilled.

Wings of Faith Ascending

On wings of faith, we rise from the ground,
In the arms of the Spirit, our hearts unbound.
Each challenge a paper, we soar through the sky,
With trust as our compass, we learn to fly.

The whisper of angels, a sweet serenade,
Guides us through shadows, where fear once played.
In the light of His love, our burdens grow light,
With wings of faith, we embrace the night.

The clouds may be heavy, the storms may rage,
Yet we find our solace, we write a new page.
In trials, we strengthen, like steel forged in fire,
With wings of faith, we climb ever higher.

Each prayer like a feather, lifts us above,
In the heavens, we dance, cradled by love.
With hearts open wide, we welcome the dawn,
On wings of faith, our spirits are drawn.

So let us ascend with our hopes as our guide,
In the arms of the sacred, in Him we confide.
With every breath taken, we choose to be free,
On wings of faith, eternally.

The Gospel of Heart's Rebirth

In the quiet of morning, the heart starts to bloom,
With whispers of love, dispelling the gloom.
From ashes of sorrow, the spirit takes flight,
In the gospel of life, we find our light.

Each heartbeat a rhythm, each breath a decree,
In the story of faith, we are truly free.
As grace washes over, we release the past,
With the song of the meek, our souls are amassed.

In the garden of kindness, we sow all our seeds,
Chasing shadows away with compassionate deeds.
Every trial transformed into lessons of gold,
In the gospel of heart's rebirth, we are bold.

With eyes full of vision, we navigate pain,
In the tapestry woven, all joy, all rain.
Renewed by the spirit, with love as our shield,
In the gospel unfolding, our fates are revealed.

As rivers of mercy flow ceaseless and wide,
We embrace one another, with faith as our guide.
In this beautiful journey, we rise and we sing,
In the gospel of heart's rebirth, we take wing.

The Invincible Heart of Faith

In the stormiest seas, our hearts will not wane,
For love is our anchor, through loss and through gain.
The invincible heart beats strong against strife,
In the armor of faith, we cherish our life.

With eyes set on heaven, we cherish each trial,
Through valleys of darkness, we walk every mile.
In the embrace of the Spirit, we learn to believe,
The invincible heart knows, it shall receive.

Through mountains and shadows, our spirits will shine,
In the light of his promise, our paths intertwine.
With faith as our fortress, we claim every dream,
The invincible heart knows hope reigns supreme.

As rivers of joy into our lives pour,
We stand hand in hand, united at core.
Each moment a blessing, together we rise,
In the invincible heart, our destiny lies.

So let us hold fast, in devotion and grace,
For the invincible heart knows no time or place.
With love as our language, we boldly proclaim,
In faith, we find strength, in love, we find flame.

Harmony of the Redeemed

In silent prayer, we gather near,
A chorus born of hope and fear.
Each heart aflame with love profound,
In unity, our souls are found.

Through trials faced, our faith remains,
In whispered grace, we break our chains.
Together, hand in hand we stand,
With open hearts, we seek the land.

The light of truth shines from above,
In every corner, peace and love.
As angels sing, we lift our voice,
In joyful praise, we make our choice.

Each life a song, each breath a hymn,
In darkest nights, our lights won't dim.
Through faith, we rise, our spirits soar,
In harmony, we seek the shore.

A promise kept, a journey's end,
To gentle hands we all commend.
In love's embrace, we find our grace,
United in this sacred space.

The Revelations Within

Within our souls, a sacred spark,
A whisper heard through shadows dark.
In quiet moments, truth unfolds,
As ancient secrets to us are told.

Each breath a chance to seek, to learn,
From silent depths, our spirits yearn.
In meditation, we find our way,
Guided by light, both night and day.

Through trials faced, we find the gold,
In every story deeply scrolled.
Revelations come as gifts divine,
In hearts awakened, love will shine.

A tapestry of life's embrace,
In every thread, a sacred trace.
United voices sing and share,
In harmony, we breathe the air.

In each dark night, dawn's hope will break,
A dance of grace for all our sakes.
Revealing joy in every sin,
For every heart holds light within.

The Burst of Heavenly Light

When dawn's embrace ignites the sky,
A burst of light, our spirits fly.
In radiant beams, we find our way,
From night's lament into the day.

Each sunlit path, a gift bestowed,
Illuminates the ways we've strode.
In shining truth, our hearts ignite,
Awakening souls with pure delight.

The warmth of love, a sacred fire,
In every heart, lifts us higher.
A symphony of joy resounds,
In heavenly grace, our peace abounds.

As shadows fade, we walk in light,
Our faith a beacon, ever bright.
Fear dissipates, we stand as one,
In this embrace, our lives begun.

Through trials faced, the light will guide,
In every heart, love will reside.
With eyes wide open, we witness so,
The burst of light that makes us grow.

Sacred Steps Toward the Divine

With every step, we seek the truth,
In whispered prayers, we find our youth.
The path may wind, the road may test,
Yet in the journey, we find rest.

Each moment spent in silent grace,
Brings us nearer to that sacred place.
The steps we take, a dance of light,
In faith, we walk through darkest night.

With hands outstretched, we reach for more,
In every heart, love's gentle core.
The promise made, our spirits soar,
In steps of faith, we find the door.

Though burdens heavy may weigh us down,
We rise again, adorned with crowns.
Each sacred step a gift to share,
In unity, we breathe the air.

Toward the Divine, our hearts combine,
In love's embrace, our spirits shine.
Together we march, through storms and sun,
In sacred steps, our journey's begun.

The Spirit's Unfolding Symphony

In the quiet morning light,
Voices rise, a holy hymn,
Whispers soar on gentle winds,
Awakening souls within.

Each note a prayer to the skies,
Every chord a sacred quest,
Boundless love in every surge,
In harmony, we find our rest.

The heartbeats sync with the stars,
A dance of grace through time and space,
In every moment, a spark divine,
The Spirit's song we embrace.

Through valleys low and mountains high,
We seek the light, we seek the way,
In union strong, the souls align,
Together as we hum and sway.

Where shadows lie, there shines a flame,
Illuminating paths unknown,
In the symphony of life, we find,
A home within the Spirit's tone.

Rebirth Beneath Heaven's Veil

In the stillness of twilight's glow,
A promise whispers on the breeze,
From ashes rise, the heart will know,
Life anew, in humble ease.

Veils of doubt are cast away,
As dawn ignites the night's refrain,
With open arms, the Spirit sways,
To greet us whole, to break the chain.

In branches bare, spring blooms anew,
Each petal speaks of grace bestowed,
With every breath, a world to view,
Rebirth unfolds on hopeful roads.

Through trials faced, we find our wings,
In sacred moments, truth reveals,
Beyond the veil, the Spirit sings,
A symphony of love that heals.

So let the old give way to light,
Beneath Heaven's veil, we rise again,
In every heart, a spark so bright,
Rebirth sings, our voices blend.

Heart's Cry for Divine Touch

In the depths of longing's sigh,
A heart reaches for the divine,
In shadows cast, the spirit cries,
For grace, for love, a sign to find.

Each tear a prayer, each breath a plea,
To feel the warmth of Heaven near,
In silence, hear the soul's decree,
A tapestry of hope and fear.

In moments lost, we seek the way,
To find the light that guides our path,
In every heart, the love will stay,
A beacon bright through trials' wrath.

With arms outstretched, we long to feel,
The touch of grace upon our skin,
In every wound, the heart can heal,
With faith, we let the journey begin.

So heed the cry, O heaven above,
For every soul deserves the light,
In faith and trust, we rise in love,
A chorus sings through darkest night.

Milton Keynes UK
Ingram Content Group UK Ltd.
UKHW020041271124
451585UK00012B/978